The Look Out! Book

A CHILD'S GUIDE TO STREET SAFETY

Cindy Blakely and Suzanne Drinkwater • Illustrated by Barbara Klunder

My name is _Justin JB_

My age is _8_

My address is _1539 JB_

My phone number is _7938188_

In an emergency, I phone _911 JB_

SCHOLASTIC INC.
New York Toronto London Auckland Sydney

THIS BOOK WOULD NOT HAVE BEEN POSSIBLE WITHOUT the generous assistance of many people. We received help from teachers, parents, child care professionals and the police. The individuals are too numerous to name, but their expertise and support were invaluable. A special thanks to Jane Somerville who believed in the project and was willing to take a risk. Last but not least, we thank our families for their patience and encouragement. — *Cindy Blakely and Suzanne Drinkwater*

Library of Congress Cataloging-in-Publication Data
Blakely, Cindy.
The look out! book.
Summary: A guidebook for children outdoors as
they deal with traffic; strange plants, animals,
and people; and other possible perils of the outdoors.
1. Children and strangers — Juvenile literature.
2. Child molesting — Prevention — Juvenile literature.
3. Traffic safety and children — Juvenile literature.
[1. Strangers.   2. Child molesting — Prevention.
3. Traffic safety.   4. Safety]   I. Drinkwater,
Suzanne.   II. Klunder, Barbara, ill.   III. Title.
HQ784.S8B58   1987   613.6   87-4347
ISBN 0-590-40962-X

12 11 10 9 8 7 6 5 4 3 2 1   7 8 9/8 0 1 2/9

Printed in the U.S.A.   23

First Scholastic printing, September 1987

Going Out

1. Always ask your mom, dad or babysitter if you can go out.

2. Tell them who you are going with and where you are going.

3. Let your parents know how they can reach you.

4. Make sure they know when you'll be home.

5. If you change your plans, always let your parents know.

Does someone always know where you are?

Always check the weather
before you go out and
think about what to wear.
Some of these people are
wearing the right clothes,
but some are not.
Can you find those who are?

BUS STOP

Rain

Where to Play

1. Ask your mom or dad where you can play safely.

2. Never play alone away from home.

3. Do not play on the road.

4. Stay away from parked cars.

5. Do not play near big machines like bulldozers, tractors and snowplows.

6. Do not go near creeks, pools or lakes without a grown-up.

7. Stay away from empty lots, alleys and construction sites.

Safe and Unsafe Places

Always choose a safe place to play.
There are two safe places in this picture
and four unsafe places.
Which two are safe and why?

Playing Safely

1. Never chase a ball or toy onto the road. Ask a grown-up for help.

2. Never cover up your eyes and ears so you can't see or hear.

3. Never play with matches, gasoline or poisons, old refrigerators or freezers, power tools like drills, chainsaws and lawnmowers, or sharp things like glass, sticks, knives and nails.

Dad!

Looking Out for Nature

Remember, never touch or eat plants without asking an adult. The plants you see here are poisonous.

poison ivy

berries

mushrooms

rhubarb leaves

lily of the valley

1. Don't touch animals you don't know, especially injured or sick ones. Ask an adult for help.
2. Stay away from fighting animals.
3. If an animal bites you, let your parents know.
4. Don't touch dog bones or animal dirt.

Going Safely

1. Look in all directions before crossing any road.
2. If possible, cross at corners.
3. Walk, never run across the street.
4. Obey traffic signs, lights and crossing guards.
5. At a crosswalk, point and wait for the traffic to stop before crossing.
6. If there are no sidewalks, walk on the left-hand side of the road, facing the traffic.

Do you look out for cars as well as signs?

28

27

29 STOP

30 DON'T play with matche[s]

26

25

Watch out for skateboarders!

24 If you're in trouble, go to the house of an adult you trust.

23 You asked an adult to get your ball from the street

The Look Out Game

1. You need markers and 1 die.
2. The object of the game is to be the first player to get home.
3. Throw the die. The highest roller begins the game. Now take turns moving your markers the number of squares shown on the die.
4. If you land on a square at the bottom of a ladder, climb up to the top.
5. If you land on a square at the top of a snake, slide down.
6. The first player to reach home by an exact throw of the die wins the game.
7. If you land on a square already taken by another player, miss your next turn.

13 You said NO to playing on train tracks!

14 Stop means Stop!

STO[P]

12

11

1 You pointed and waited at a crosswalk.

2

1. Obey traffic signs and safety rules.

2. Check your bike. Does it have good tires, a light, a horn and reflectors?

3. Always watch for cars on roads and driveways.

4. Look out for other people and animals.

5. Learn the hand signals.

   RIGHT TURN   STOP!   LEFT TURN

6. If you ride on the road, ride in single file on the right-hand side, going with the cars.

7. Do not do stunts. Never ride two on a bike.

Do you walk your bike across the road?

Staying Safe

1. Always ask your parents before you go anywhere with anybody.

2. Know what plans your parents have made for you. If your plans change, be sure your parents know.

3. Unless your parents know, never get into a car, never go into anyone's house, and never accept gifts, candy or money.

4. It's unusual for adults to ask kids for help. It's best to stay away.

5. Be careful if a grown-up asks for directions. Always stand well back.

6. Stay with your friends. There is safety in numbers. Play together and stay together.

7. If a friend or grown-up asks you to do something you don't think is right, say NO.

8. Remember, if something feels bad or scary, get away and tell someone you trust.

Can you say no to a grown-up?

Asking for Help

Here are some people and places you can go to for help.

What If...

1. You are lost.

2. Nobody is home.

3. A friend or animal is hurt.

4. Your pet runs away and climbs up a tree.

5. Your friend's mom wants to take you home earlier than planned.

6. You're alone at home, and there's a problem.

7. Your babysitter lets you do something your parents don't normally let you do.

8. Somebody gives you a gift, and you don't know why.

What would you do? Can you and your parents think of other "What If's"?

9. You are asked to do something you don't think is right.

10. Someone touches you where you don't want to be touched.

11. You are asked to keep a secret from your parents.

12. Something strange happens to you or a friend, and you're afraid to talk about it.

13. Someone other than your parents or babysitter wants to pick you up at school.

14. Your parents are not living together. The parent you are visiting does not want to take you home.

Looking Out for Kids

About the Authors

CINDY BLAKELY is the mother of three. In addition, she is a social worker with special experience in Child Welfare. Currently she works for the Toronto Board of Education as a school social worker. SUZANNE DRINKWATER is also a mother of three. She has worked in many areas in book publishing and is presently an acquisitions editor for a Canadian publishing house. Both authors are Block Parents and executive members of their school associations.

BARBARA KLUNDER illustrated *The Dennis Lee Big Book* and has won numerous illustration awards in Canada and the United States. She is the mother of one.